MONKEY
Gains His Powers

Written and Illustrated by **WILL STRONG**

Translated by **ROBERT NOORDA**

ThunderStone Books
Las Vegas, Nevada

Illustrations © Will Strong, 2014
Text © Will Strong and Robert Noorda, 2014
Translated by Robert Noorda

Edited, designed, typset, written, and project managed by Robert and Rachel Noorda at ThunderStone Books. Printed and bound by IngramSpark.

This book may not be reproduced in whole or in part, in any form or by any means, electronic or mechanical, including photocopying, recording, or by any information storage and retrieval system now known or hereafter invented, without written permission from the publisher.

978-1-63411-002-0 (ISBN 13)

This one is for you Tiff. You are the best for me. —WS

Long ago in ancient China, there was a magic stone on top of a high mountain.
很久以前,在古代中国,在一座高山上有一块神奇的石头。

One night a great storm came to the mountain. The wind blew, the rain poured, and the lightning struck. Crack!

一天晚上,一场大风暴来到山上。刮起一阵大风,下起了大雨,一声雷响。咔嚓!

A monkey was born from the stone!
从石头里生出来一只猴子!

"My name is Sun Wukong. I am brave and fierce," he said to the heavens.
"我叫孙悟空。我骁勇善战,"他朝天上说。

Sun Wukong climbed down from the mountain top to explore the world. After traveling for several hours he met a group of monkeys drinking from a stream.

孙悟空从山上爬下来探索世界。他走了几个小时后,遇到一群猴子在小河边饮水。

"If someone could find the source of this stream, we would make him our king!" said the monkeys.

"谁能找到这条小河的源头,我们就让谁做我们的王!"猴子们说。

Sun Wukong followed the stream up the dangerous mountain path. He found a beautiful valley where the stream began.

孙悟空顺着小河边的山间小路一直走,最后在一个美丽的山谷找到了小河的源头。

"Friends," said Sun Wukong, "I have found the source of the stream. It is a golden valley filled with fruit and room for us to play."

"朋友们,"孙悟空说,"我找到了小河的源头,那是一个金色的山谷,长满了水果,并且有足够我们能玩的空间。"

"And you shall be our king!" cried the monkeys together.

"你就当我们的王吧!"猴子们同声喊道。

Life was good for the Monkey King. He ruled his subjects justly and all the monkeys lived in peace.

猴子王的生活很顺利。他公正地统治臣民,他们在一起过着和平的生活。

But Sun Wukong knew that it could not last. He knew that someday he must die.
可是,孙悟空知道不能继续这样。他知道他总有一天会死。

"I will not die," said Sun Wukong. "I will discover a way to live forever."
"我不要死,"孙悟空说,"我要找到长生不老的办法。"

So the Monkey King left the other monkeys in search of eternal life.
于是,猴子王就离开了其他的猴子去寻找长生不老的秘密。

On his journey he found a magic staff.
他在旅程中先找到了一个魔法棒。

After many weeks of travel Sun Wukong came to the home of a great sage.
又过了好几个星期,孙悟空到达了一位伟大圣人的家。

"Please," said Sun Wukong, "you are a great and wise sage. I do not want to die. Teach me how to conquer Death."

"拜托,"孙悟空说,"您是一位又伟大又有智慧的圣人。我不想死。请教我征服死亡的方法。"

The great sage answered, "I can teach you many tricks. But in the end you must face Death alone. Let us begin your training."

伟大圣人回答说,"我能教你好几个技巧,不过,你必须自己面对死亡。我们开始你的训练吧。"

First, the great sage taught the Monkey King to walk on the clouds.
伟大圣人先教猴子王翻觔斗云。

Next, the great sage taught the Monkey King to use his magic staff to perform many tricks.
接着,伟大圣人又教孙悟空使用魔法棒的技巧。

Last, the great sage taught the Monkey King to master the 72 transformations, though he had difficulty hiding his tail.

最后,圣人教猴子王学会了七十二变,尽管他的尾巴不容易藏起来。

After many weeks of training the great sage announced, "Sun Wukong, king of monkeys, your training is complete."

经过好几个星期的训练,伟大圣人说,"孙悟空,猴子的王,你的训练终于结束了。"

"And when I meet Death," said Sun Wukong "I will be ready. I am brave and bold. I will defeat Death and I will live forever."

"当我遇到死亡的时候,"孙悟空说,"我会准备好的。我很勇敢,也很胆大。我会打败死亡而长生不老。"

Then Sun Wukong, king of the monkeys, left to seek his fate.
孙悟空,猴子的王,之后就离开去寻求他的明天。

Begin your own journey.
www.thunderstonebooks.com

www.ingramcontent.com/pod-product-compliance
Lightning Source LLC
Chambersburg PA
CBHW051354070526
44584CB00025B/3765